WHOOSH!
The Story of Snowboarding

Lisa Trumbauer

Contents

Rigby®
A Harcourt Achieve Imprint

www.Rigby.com
1-800-531-5015

What Is Snowboarding?

Imagine you're **surfing** over a wave, then, *whoosh!* You're flying through the air, twisting through a **skateboarding** trick before landing on a snowy path below. You wouldn't be surfing or skateboarding. You'd be snowboarding!

skateboarding

surfing

Snowboarding is like surfing, skateboarding, and **skiing** all in one. You stand on a board just like you do when you are on a surfboard or skateboard, and you slide on snow just like you do on skis.

snowboarding

How Did Snowboarding Get Started?

No one knows who invented snowboarding, but in 1965, Sherman Poppen watched his daughter ride down a hill, standing on her sled. This led him to create something new. He put the words "snow" and "surf" together and called his new snowboard a snurfer.

early snowboard

In the 1970s, Jake Burton Carpenter added rubber straps to the snowboard. This made it easier for a snowboarder's feet to turn the board. He also made snowboards weigh less and taught people how to do the sport safely.

snowboard of the 1970s

Where Do People Snowboard?

Snowy hills, ski slopes, and even snowboarding parks are different places to snowboard. Ski slopes have lifts that take you to mountaintops. Then you slide down. Parks have **halfpipes**, or deep slopes, with high sides that snowboarders like to use for tricks and turns. There's even a halfpipe team event in the Winter Olympics!

About 20 years ago, most ski slopes didn't allow snowboarders. Today, one out of every five people on a ski slope is a snowboarder.

snowboarder, sailing and twisting down a slope

What Safety Gear Do Snowboarders Use?

You want to be safe while you are snowboarding, so you should begin by snowboarding on small hills. Wear safety **gear**, like a helmet, in case you fall.

snowboarder safely falling

If you feel like you are falling, bend your knees and try to sit down. It's important to protect yourself, so you'll need a pair of wrist guards and knee pads, too.

Snowboarders can move fast, and can crash into the ground, a tree, or another snowboarder. That's why it's important to learn snowboard safety.

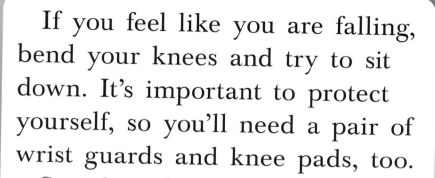

helmet

wrist guards

knee pads

What Should Snowboarders Know About Avalanches?

Snowboarders always need to watch for **avalanches**. An avalanche is a real danger on a mountain and can happen quickly. An avalanche happens when a new layer of snow doesn't stick to the layer beneath it. The new snow collapses or slides down the mountain in one large pile. That's an avalanche!

How Most Avalanches Happen

before

during

after

avalanche

When someone gets caught in an avalanche, groups of people called search and rescue teams quickly try to find them. The teams use long, thin poles to feel under the deep snow.

search and rescue team after an avalanche

Why Should Snowboarders Take Lessons?

You should take a lesson before you try snowboarding because it is a sport that you will need to practice. Your teacher will show you how to take baby steps, use your heels to slide, and turn on flat places. Wear waterproof pants and gloves to keep you warm and dry.

snowboarding lesson

Practice as often as you can. When you're ready, you can add new turns and jumps. In time you'll be great!

Glossary

avalanche big pile of snow that slides down a mountain

gear special clothes and tools

halfpipe a *u*-shaped tube that snowboarders use to do tricks

skateboarding riding or doing tricks on a short, narrow board with wheels that people ride on the ground

skiing standing on a pair of long, narrow boards that people use to slide across snow while holding poles

surfing standing or sitting on a long, narrow board that people use to ride on the ocean waves